Aliaa is an American university of Sharjah graduate with Banking background. She is a poet and free spirit individual.

Aliaa Dongula

Live it Right Tips

Austin Macauley Publishers™
London • Cambridge • New York • Sharjah

Copyright © Aliaa Dongula 2022

The age category suitable for the books' contents has been classified and defined in accordance to the Age Classification System issued by the National Media Council.

ISBN – 9789948817406 – (Paperback)
ISBN – 9789948817413 – (E-Book)

Application Number: MC-10-01-2866155
Age Classification: E

First Published 2022
AUSTIN MACAULEY PUBLISHERS FZE
Sharjah Publishing City
P.O Box [519201]
Sharjah, UAE
www.austinmacauley.ae
+971 655 95 202

I dedicate this book to my family and my
loved ones.

Tip No. 1

Clear your mind. Take a deep breath and exhale all your negative thoughts.

Tip No. 2

Appreciate every minute of your life, as every minute passed will not come again.

Tip No. 3

Have faith; what you desire will sooner or later be in your hands. What comes easy goes easy.

Tip No. 4

Recite what you want daily. As you say it, your
unconscious mind will believe it, manifesting
what your soul desires.

Tip No. 5

Believe everything will come on the right time,
aligning with your soul purpose and happiness.

Tip No. 6

Be kind and forgiving as a white heart will be
filled with light and positivity.

<u>Tip No. 7</u>

Attract what you want by feeling it actually
happening – nothing is impossible.

<u>Tip No. 8</u>

Imagining what you want will give you a
sensational feeling for a couple of minutes,
which will get you closer to your desires.

<u>Tip No. 9</u>

Acceptance is the first guideline and the first
step in reaching where you want to be.

Tip No. 10

Never give up hope, the universe will give you signs that will keep you going on.

Tip No. 11

Having everything is not happiness, appreciating what you have is.

Tip No. 12

Give money to the poor, you will definitely feel good about yourself.

Tip No. 13

Give with no expectations; expectations can
sometimes destroy you. Be reasonable
and hopeful.

Tip No. 14

Treat people the way you want to be treated, it's
a reflection of yourself.

Tip No. 15

Laugh more often; laughing changes your mood.

Tip No. 16

Eat Chocolates, but to help maintain that weight have a dark chocolate. Eating it increases your happiness level.

Tip No. 17

If you are feeling angry, frustrated, and annoyed, don't keep it inside. If possible, find an empty spot and scream, push all your negative energy out. You will feel good, trust me.

Tip No. 18

Play with your child or any child if you don't have one of your own, your heart will be full of joy.

Tip No. 19

Smile more often; by smiling you attract positive attitudes.

Tip No. 20

Do something you enjoy every day even for five minutes, it will make a difference.

Tip No. 21

Don't stress and if you do, take a break and breathe, then continue what you were doing.

Tip No. 22

Life is a one-time shot, make it count.

Tip No. 23

Count your blessings, you will see that you
are rich.

Tip No. 24

Save one dirham every day; after a while, you will
have enough for minor emergencies.

Tip No. 25

Never forget you have a purpose in life.

Tip No. 26

Thrive to always be the best, without hurting others mentally.

Tip No. 27

Spending time with your family will make you appreciate small things.

Tip No. 28

Choose your friends wisely. Having the right friends helps you through your journey.

Tip No. 29

Nothing is impossible, make sure you say that every day.

Tip No. 30

Work hard, it will pay off.

Tip No. 31

Love yourself before you can love someone, as
this love will be balanced.

Tip No. 32

Don't expect all who are around you to think and
feel like you but try to adapt and be flexible, so
that you and others can find a common ground.

Tip No. 33

Believe in yourself, you deserve love.

Tip No. 34

Make sure not to over-give to any person, to not feel less appreciated. Give equally to what you get.

Tip No. 35

You are beautiful inside no matter how you look outside, believe it.

Tip No. 36

Exercise or just walk gives you a positive push to what comes next.

Tip No. 37

Give your body enough sleep. This will help you to accomplish your daily duties with a happier attitude.

Tip No. 38

Don't keep grudges; if something is bothering you, be honest and say it to avoid future consequences.

Tip No. 39

Nothing stays the same, things will change to the better. Believe it will.

Tip No. 40

It's all about the mindset, you control it. It comes with practice.

Tip No. 41

Life is not easy, so don't complicate it.

Tip No. 42

Acknowledge your weakness and work on it, we are not perfect. No one is.

Tip No. 43

Put yourself in others' shoes and think before
you speak, words that come out can never
be returned.

Tip No. 44

When angry, count to five and then think is it
worth it what made you mad.

Tip No. 45

Everything happens for a reason. Just make sure
you understand and learn from all
your experiences.

Tip No. 46

Don't play with people's feelings or Karma will get you. What goes around comes around.

Tip No. 47

Try every day to be a better version of you.

Tip No. 48

Forgive and forget, we all make mistakes. But learn from them.

Tip No. 49

Keep your enemy close, and not everyone is
your friend.

Tip No. 50

If you have enemies, it means you are
successful. Continue what you are doing, no one
can stop you from getting to your goal.

Tip No. 51

The power of love can help you to overcome the
cruelness of life. The best rush that a person
can undergo.

Tip No. 52

Appreciate the efforts of those who are there for you in hard times more than sweet times.

Tip No. 53

Love is the melody of harmony and the beat of glee.

Tip No. 54

No place for the weak. Survival of the fittest.

Tip No. 55

Money isn't everything. It's the empathy and care that resembles one's worthiness.

Tip No. 56

Have values, only then you will know what direction you should go in.

Tip No. 57

Have healthy boundaries in all your relationships; whether friendships or love relationships.

Tip No. 58

We are all blessed in one way or another.

Tip No. 59

It is the tiny things that make a difference and leave behind a huge impact.

Tip No. 60

Look around you, observe the beauty of life, never look up to hate but look down to appreciate, then and only then you'll treasure what you have.

Tip No. 61

It is us humans who create our inner peace and happiness, it's us who drive and crave for a better and a brighter tomorrow.

Tip No. 62

Life is short, there is no time to waste. Indulge your senses, pamper your precious, worthy self.

Tip No. 63

Accept your flaws, embrace your weakness, and love yourself unconditionally.

Tip No. 64

Always give the benefit of the doubt until proven otherwise, don't judge; it's our creator who knows our true intentions.

Tip No. 65

Inner beauty never fades but outer beauty does. The personality does matter.

Tip No. 66

When it's time to move on, don't look back. You have enjoyed the good memories, learn from the bad ones.

Tip No. 67

Share your wisdom. Some people do need it.

Tip No. 68

It is funny how someone's life can transform in a friction of a second. How feelings can evolve or dissolve. Make sure you are always making the right choices. Don't rush, take your sweet time.

Tip No. 69

It is strange how one word can lift us up and one word can tear us down.

Tip No. 70

Be strong no matter how many times life brings you down, no matter how many pretenders find their way into your life.

Tip No. 71

The world is full of strangers, full of haters, but it's those incidents and situations that unveil hidden masks, that reveal concealed emotions.

Tip No. 72

A day will come when all your worries will end as for every beginning there must be an end.

Tip No. 73

Speak up and never be afraid to express. Enjoy life as if it's your last day.

Tip No. 74

Never judge a book by its cover. What people wear does not define them. Get to know them before judging.

Tip No. 75

Nothing wrong with kind people, just don't take advantage of them. Not any one being kind to you wants something from you.
Don't generalize.

Tip No. 76

Try different tasks until you find where your talent lies.

Tip No. 77

Never forget any situation where someone stood by you as these people are true from the inside.

Tip No. 78

You don't need someone's approval to feel good about yourself. You are worthy. You are unique and special in your own way.

Tip No. 79

No one will take the best care of you than yourself. Sometimes, you need to put you first; that is not being selfish, that called being living.

Tip No. 80

Try once or twice to use a public transportation. You will not only have an experience but you will also appreciate what you have and see that not everyone can afford a car.

Tip No. 81

You cannot change someone but through your actions, you can alter some of their behaviors toward you.

Tip No. 82

You cannot change someone but through your actions, you can alter some of their behaviors toward you.

Tip No. 83

Nature is one of the wonders of life. If you feel down, just take a walk around the nearest garden or listen to your favorite music while watching the waves of the water slide.

Tip No. 84

Ask about your old friends and relatives from time to time, you will feel good about it as you are initiating and maintaining the bond between both of you. Eventually, they will do the same.

Tip No. 85

If you love someone, try your best to make it work and if they don't reciprocate it, take a step back and observe what they do. Then you will know what you mean to them.

Tip No. 86

They say you will appreciate it once it's gone. Why do you have to go through pain to do so? Appreciate all the good as it's rare nowadays.

Tip No. 87

Patience is not easy but through time and different situations you go through, it will get easier. Good things take time to come.

Tip No. 88

If you can't express your feelings, write it down. It helps you to lessen the magnitude of what you are going through.

Tip No. 89

Taking care of a pet can assist you in having responsibility toward other living things.

Tip No. 90

Always believe something miraculous will happen at any second. Thinking positive attracts positive.

Tip No. 91

Write it down how you want your life to be. Write it and say it daily with a positive attitude. You are capable of creating your own desires.

Tip No. 92

Never fear from making mistakes as these mistakes make us what we are today.

Tip No. 93

Give excuses to people's behaviors. You don't know what led them to do so. Never misunderstand someone unless you confront them and get a clear message why they did what they did.

Tip No. 94

Seeing repeated numbers is a sign of transformation and opportunities are heading your way. Be positive, everything is possible.

Tip No. 95

Treat yourself to expensive things from time to time after accomplishing every objective you achieve. You deserve it.

Tip No. 96

Don't keep on saving money all the time and deprive yourself from enjoying your life. Maybe tomorrow, you will not be part of it.

Tip No. 97

To get the courage to face your issues, your mirror is the best practice.

Tip No. 98

While you are doubting your capabilities, there are others that admire you and wish that they were you. Never doubt yourself, you are what you want to be.

Tip No. 99

If you do apologize a lot, that is not necessarily bad, it just means that you do care a lot. Try to always be balanced, don't apologize for the things you did which you thought were right. This is your point of view.

Tip No. 100

Not everything said is true, make sure from
the source. Gossips are perceived and changed
through the channel of word of mouth.

Tip No. 101

Never give up even if you fail millions of times.
One day, you will be a winner and you will make
yourself proud of you.

Tip No. 102

Overcome the fear of change, as some situations
in life force you to change, and that would be the
best thing to do – to adapt.

Tip No. 103

Being fat or thin should matter only to you. As long as you are confident and love the way you look, people's opinions do not matter until you let them.

Tip No. 104

Don't compare your life to others'. They might not have what you have.

Tip No. 105

Be transparent. Be easy to deal with, you live once. Why make it difficult for you and others?

Tip No. 106

Happy moments don't last, so enjoy every little bit of these moments. And make sure you create your own happy moments.

Tip No. 107

People will envy smart people as not everyone gets it from the first time. If you are smart, be grateful, not everyone is.

Tip No. 108

When you wake up, that means you are given another chance to correct your wrongdoings and create a new agenda. Be creative.

Tip No. 109

Don't take revenge. It might feel good at the beginning but eventually, you will see yourself as bad as they were. Let God and the universe take it for you.

Tip No. 110

When you think deeply, you will see that you were not wrong. You did what you thought was right at that moment.

Tip No. 111

We are humans not robots, we don't control all our emotions. It is okay to cry.

Tip No. 112

Respect different opinions as we are not all the same. If we were, trust me, it would be a boring world.

Tip No. 113

Pray more often, pray the way you know how to pray and ask the Lord for all you desire. Have faith. You will get what you want, just be patient.

Tip No. 114

If you do something wrong, do apologize and make sure you don't repeat the same mistakes. Not everyone has the capability to forgive.

Tip No. 115

Time is the best healer. Give them time if they pushed you away. If they do care, they will come back.

Tip No. 116

If you are nice and kind, that does not mean everyone is. You will know who you are dealing with by observing their behaviors.

Tip No. 117

Accept that certain things cannot be changed. And not everyone can be saved.

Tip No. 118

It takes years to be where you want to be. Getting there is not easy but maintaining it will be easier.

Tip No. 119

Do what makes you happy and distract yourself from negative thoughts. Watch a movie, or read a book.

Tip No. 120

Learn another language or even explore other cultures' habits and their famous dishes. Try new things.

Tip No. 121

What does not kill you makes you stronger. What hurts you the most makes you a wiser person.

Tip No. 122

If it makes you better to break a glass or hit a mattress or scream out loud, do it. No one can feel what you feel.

Tip No. 123

Fake it until you make it. Pretend and practice what you want, you will get there eventually and it will look and feel natural then.

Tip No. 124

Take care of your health and skin. Eat healthy, eat smaller portions, and have core meals. Drink water a lot, it is good for your health and skin.

Tip No. 125

When taking care of others, remember you are human too. It is nice to be taken care of from time to time.

Tip No. 126

Learn to be assertive when needed, some situations need a bold move and a straightforward response.

Tip No.127

When someone takes out time to do something for you or help you out, be nice, they are not forced to do it.

Tip No.128

If you are a short-tempered individual, control your anger by taking a deep breath and do not say a word. Think about the whole situation one more time before you make any response.

Tip No.129

Think like a boss and act like a prince. You are who you are by the way you act.

Tip No. 130

A smile to a stranger can give them a sense of happiness till the end of the day.

Tip No. 131

Having connections is different than having friends. Real friends are there for the whole picture.

Tip No. 132

Don't overthink. Answers will fall in line and things will happen the way they are supposed to happen. What you can't control, let the universe take control over it.

Tip No. 133

Let yourself shine out there, nothing will bring you down. You are the driver of your journey.

Tip No. 134

Don't lose hope. As long as you are a breathing soul, everything is possible.

Tip No. 135

No one knows you better than you. Make yourself a priority, others come next.

Tip No. 136

Sometimes, what you desire doesn't come true
as there are better things heading your way.
Believe so.

Tip No. 137

When you find food in your refrigerator, be
thankful, some people can't afford to buy food.

Tip No. 138

As long as you have a bed to sleep on and a
blanket to keep you warm, be grateful. Some
people are homeless.

Tip No. 139

Don't complain. Either solve it or live with it and
adapt. Complaining just makes it
more complicated.

Tip No. 140

Help others with no hidden agenda. Your good
deeds come back to you as solutions to
your problems.

Tip No. 141

Always remember, no one can care for you more
than your family. Value your quality time
with them.

Tip No. 142

When doors close, new doors open.
Opportunities are endless. Never give up and
aim higher every time.

Tip No. 143

Moralities and ethics are the ground rule for
every situation. Don't be biased to any situation,
be true to what is wrong and right.

Tip No. 144

Solve your problems rather than running from
them. They will not disappear by themselves.
Solving more problems will widen your scope
of thinking.

Tip No. 145

Do charity work. Not only will you feel good about yourself, you will be a giving hand for a needy person.

Tip No. 146

Everyone's existence is essential. You play an important role in this world whether you see it or not.

Tip No. 147

Take time for yourself and evaluate where do you stand. Note down your drawbacks and work on them to be a better person.

Tip No. 148

Time never stops. Accomplish as much as you can in the shortest time possible. Add value to yourself first then to the society.

Tip No. 149

To make a difference in someone's life, you don't need to be a superhero. Just be there when they need you.

Tip No. 150

When you are in a toxic relationship, take yourself out of the equation. You are hurting yourself before hurting the other party.

Tip No. 151

Tell the truth no matter how harsh the truth is.
Lies tend to be discovered sooner or later.

Tip No. 152

Be an example for others to follow. Don't be a
doormat for others to step on.

Tip No. 153

With the right tools and the right company, you
will get to where you are supposed to be with
full control.